Christmas in Britain

Christmas Around the World
From World Book

World Book, Inc.
a Scott Fetzer company
Chicago　London　Sydney　Toronto

Contents

The editors gratefully acknowledge the cooperation of the British Tourist Authority.

World Book, Inc.
525 W. Monroe
Chicago, IL 60661

ISBN: 0-7166-0874-x
LC: 96-60211

Printed in Mexico.

4 5 6 7 8 9 10 99 98 97

One Thousand Years of Christmas

No other people have ever observed Christmas as lustily as the English—and they have been celebrating it for well over one thousand years! According to legend, King Arthur spent Christmas at York in 521 with "jocund (merry) guests, minstrels, gleemen, harpers, pipe-players, jugglers, and dancers." An English chronicle of 1736 claimed that King Arthur, his clergy, all his nobility, soldiers, and neighbors spent the holidays in mirth, jollity, and drinking.

Ever since, except for a brief period of Puritan rule, vigorous feasting and merrymaking have been the order of the season. Even the word **Christmas** comes from **Christes** (Christ) and **Masse**, an old English word for feast or festival. Once, Christmas was celebrated for twelve days each year, each day having its own name and special observances.

Early invaders of England came from many parts of Europe, and they brought their own customs with them. Christianity arrived in England in the sixth century, and eventually Christmas became a merry fusion of old and new, of pagan and Christian rituals.

A Puritan ban on Christmas in the mid-1600's ended after the monarchy was restored in 1660, and the holiday then became more spiritual. In the 1800's, the Victorian Era added some new touches, including the Christmas tree and Christmas cards. Christmas in Britain is a quieter time now than in days of old, but it is still a festival of joy, rich with tradition. And though the incredible banquets, jousting tournaments, and boisterous revelry of the Middle Ages may be long gone, many remnants of colorful old-time Yuletide customs are still practiced.

Britain announces the holiday season with music—concerts; pealing, clamorous bells; and multitudes of carols. In addition to the wealth of classic Christmas music that is part of the British heritage, new carols are always being added by contemporary composers.

Christmas has always inspired writers and poets, too, and some of the liveliest examples of Christmas literature have come from England. William Shakespeare, John Milton, Robert Herrick, Lord Tennyson, William Makepeace Thackeray, Anthony Trollope, Christina Rossetti, George Bernard Shaw, Dylan Thomas—these and many more have given us the flavor, taste, and sound of British Christmastide.

Charles Dickens, sometimes called "Father Christmas himself," toured England and America giving readings of **A Christmas Carol.** Eager audiences stood in long lines in freezing weather to hear him. Washington Irving was an American, but he lived in England for seventeen years and captured the essence of English Christmas in his Sketchbook.

In this book we have attempted to bring you a panorama of Christmas in Britain—past and present. Included are suggestions for projects to make, carols to sing, and Christmas foods for your table. We hope that you will find it entertaining, and may you and yours share the happiest of holidays—a true British Christmas.

Sights and Sounds of Yuletide London

Four great bronze lions guard Trafalgar Square in the center of London. High above them, on a towering granite column, looms the famous statue of Lord Nelson. A pair of splendid fountains fill the early evening air with mist. And between them stands a magnificent tall Christmas tree, its slender tip adorned with a glowing white star.

Lights twinkle on the tree as the chilly breeze stirs its dark green branches. Except for the lights, it looks as if it might still be growing in the cold Norwegian forest where it was born. The giant spruce is a gift from Norway. Each year since World War II, the city of Oslo has sent a tree to the city of London.

On this night, December 22, the tree looked down upon a tightly packed crowd of hushed and waiting people. Children were everywhere, wandering through the throng, climbing on Nelson's column, and almost obscuring the lions. Directly in front of the tree, two rows of schoolchildren watched their leader expectantly. They formed one of the many bands of carolers who gather there nightly in the weeks before Christmas. The teacher raised her hand giving the signal for the children to begin.

"Joy to the world!" A small girl in a bright red woolen cap added her clear voice to those of the other carolers. As she sang, 10-year-old Elizabeth peered across the square at the lions. Her younger brothers, Tony and Peter, had told her to look for them, and—yes, there they were! Crouched between the paws of the nearest lion, the boys were making horrible faces at her. She swallowed a giggle, not missing a note. Somewhere

Father and daughter watch the glowing lights of fountains and Christmas tree in London's Trafalgar Square. Throughout the Christmas season, carolers of all ages perform nightly at the tree.

Traffic whizzes past and crowds line up to view the display windows at Harrods, London's famous department store. The block-long building is a Christmas display in itself, with its thousands of shimmering lights.

Harrods' great food halls provide every imaginable kind of delicacy under high-vaulted, gleaming tile ceilings, including Christmas venison and birds.

in the crowd her parents were watching and listening, too, as Elizabeth and her class caroled enthusiastically.

When the notes of the final noel had drifted over the square, Elizabeth located her mother and father. Together they persuaded the reluctant boys to come down from the lion, and the family set off on a walk through London's streets to see the Christmas decorations. Traditional gaslit arcades tempted passers-by with glittering displays, shop windows offered holiday panoramas, and lighted Christmas trees brightened many storefronts. Harrods, an entire block long, was completely outlined in white lights. Elizabeth thought it looked like an enchanted castle.

The boys tugged at their parents' sleeves. "Let's go inside!" they begged.

Harrods is an immense store—a shopping center all in one building. There are more than 200 departments, and maps are available to help customers find what they are looking for. To Peter and Tony, it seemed like a giant Aladdin's cave, full of dazzling arrays of books, clothes, perfume, furniture, silver, leather goods—even a zoo!

Hand in hand, the Bushnells wandered slowly up one aisle and down another, staring in awe—and sniffing—at the palatial food halls. Vast selections of meats, fish, poultry, fruits, and vegetables vied for attention with pastries, yummy cakes, and luscious candies. The children dragged their parents to the third floor, where the toy department did its best to fulfill the wistful dreams of wide-eyed youngsters. There was even a separate section just for "cuddly" toys.

Earlier that day, Mother and the children had visited Selfridges, another large London store. There they finished most of their Christmas shopping, and joined the spectators on the sidewalk admiring the window scenes. Each year Selfridges' windows present a different Christmas story. This year it was *Pinocchio*, with a whole doll-sized village full of characters from that old tale.

And, as a special treat, the family feasted on gooey ice cream concoctions at Fortnum & Mason. Elizabeth loved that shop—it was especially intriguing during the holidays. Thick red carpeting muffled footsteps; pyramids of delicious things to eat caught the eye; and busy clerks scurried about dressed in festive red jackets. The rest of the year the clerks

dressed more soberly in morning coats and striped trousers.

Now night had fallen, and it was time to go home. The Bushnells lived in a suburb of London, a short train ride from the city. As they walked up the steep High Street of their town, they stopped for a few minutes to listen to a group of adult carolers. Dressed in colorful costumes, the singers stood in a semicircle around the lighted doorway of an old inn.

Elizabeth felt like singing along with them, but their voices blended so beautifully that she thought she had better just hum quietly. Smiling

Last-minute shoppers fill the streets and sidewalks of a London street just a few short days before Christmas. Over their heads sparkling holiday lights set the mood.

Bright and early the next morning the family gathered in the kitchen to help Mother make the Christmas pudding. ...They all took turns stirring, each one making a wish as they did so.

people hurried by, laden with packages, bunches of glossy green holly, and Christmas trees.

"When do we get our own tree?" Tony asked. "Can't we buy it tonight?"

Dad shook his head and guided them off in the direction of their house. "We've all had enough excitement for one day," he laughed. "Tree shopping can wait until tomorrow."

Bright and early the next morning, the family gathered in the kitchen after breakfast to help Mother make the Christmas pudding. Even Dad was there; his Christmas holiday started the night before. Mum brought out measuring cups and spoons and a large bowl. Elizabeth ran to get eggs, flour, fat, and spices, and the boys climbed up to get the raisins from a cupboard shelf.

"Stop eating those raisins," Mum cried, suddenly noticing their rapid disappearance. "There won't be enough left for the pudding."

She quickly measured out all of the ingredients into the bowl, and then passed around the bowl and a big spoon. They all took turns stirring, each one making a wish as they did so. Then the children carefully wrapped a five-penny piece in paper and dropped it into the mixture.

"Whoever finds this coin at Christmas dinner will have good luck," Peter chanted, as Mum wrapped the pudding in a cloth and set it in a large pot to boil.

"Why is it called 'plum pudding' when there aren't any plums in it?" Elizabeth asked.

"I think they used to use prunes," Mum answered. "Dried plums. We use raisins nowadays instead. That is, if two small boys haven't eaten them all up first."

"Who wants to go with me to look for a Christmas tree?" Dad asked. "I'll need help in choosing a good one."

"Me, me!" Tony yelled. "I want to go!"

"Everyone can go," Mum told him. "We have to buy a turkey, too, and I still have a few presents to get."

The Bushnells walked into town, the children skipping along beside their parents. Overhead on the main streets, Christmas decorations strung on wires quivered in the morning air. There were giant, lacy snowflakes, and gay pennants that looked like ancient tapestries. Every shop window along the way seemed to be stuffed full of things to buy.

Elizabeth and the boys spotted the toyshop. Running on ahead, they pressed their noses against the glass and stared longingly at the fascinating wealth of treasures spread about within. An electric train ran clickety-clack on a circular track. Heaped around it were dolls of every size and description, stacks of games, and a whole regiment of tin toy soldiers.

Inside the store, the children found even more alluring offerings. Wooden rocking horses stood on the floor ready for small riders, and there was a splendid dollhouse completely furnished in Victorian style, down to the tiniest tufted red velvet sofa. Teddy bears and other stuffed animals sat on shelves and counters. With difficulty, Mum and Dad managed to pry the children loose, and aimed them toward the butcher's.

There, rows of pale plucked turkeys and geese hung upside down from the walls, and the jolly, white-smocked butcher rushed up to wait on his new customers.

Two boys shopping for family Christmas presents consider the options in a dazzling storefront display.

"Good morning, good morning!" he
beamed. "Come to buy your Christmas dinner, have you? What will it
be? A fat goose, or a plump, fresh
turkey?"

"We'll have a turkey this year,"
Mum smiled back at him. "That one
over there looks just right."

The butcher bustled about weighing
and wrapping her choice, and handed
it over to Dad, wishing them all a
Happy Christmas.

"One more errand," Mum said,
leading the family up the street to
another small shop. "But you'll all
have to stay outside. I have some
special things to buy."

No one minded. As they waited,
Dad and the children amused themselves by looking at the interesting
objects displayed in the shop's window. Mum wasn't inside very long,
and when she returned she was carrying several packages, all gaily wrapped.
Elizabeth and her brothers wanted
to know what they were, but Mum
just smiled mysteriously.

"You'll know soon enough," she informed them. "Now we'll go look for a tree."

Outside the greengrocer's, a small forest of cut fir trees stood on the sidewalk. Most of the trees were spruce, the British favorite for Christmas decorating. After comparing the virtues of a dozen or so, the Bushnells chose a thickly-branched, dark-needled tree about five feet tall. Dad was carrying the turkey, so Peter, Tony, and Elizabeth offered to take the tree. Getting a good grip on its trunk, they marched along, making sure the branches didn't scrape the ground. On the way home, the family stopped briefly at a church near their house so the children could see the crib, or manger scene. Leaving the tree outside, they tiptoed in and found the miniature Nativity scene just inside the church door. Elizabeth was charmed by the tiny figures of Joseph and Mary and the Infant Jesus. Peter and Tony liked

the camels and donkeys best, and the Three Wise Men in their richly colored robes.

Late that afternoon Dad called the children in from playing out-of-doors; it was time to trim the tree. They raced in, red-cheeked from the nippy air.

"Hang up your coats," Mum reminded them. "And try not to step on the cat." That furry animal was busily weaving itself around their ankles, happy to see them again.

Mum dug out boxes of ornaments, and Dad strung the colored lights. The tree had been set firmly into a bucket of sand and placed in a corner of the living room. It filled the whole room with its fresh, woodsy scent.

On went shiny balls, glittery butterflies, and birds. Toy soldiers and little toy drums made of molded glass were also hung from the branches. The boys then sat on the floor making garlands of brightly colored, twisted streamers, and Elizabeth unreeled

A visit to a Christmas manger scene, such as this one in the crypt of the Canterbury Cathedral, is an annual holiday custom for many British families.

This elaborately decorated tree and a generous array of presents stand ready to be discovered by the children on Christmas morning. A glowing fire in the hearth sends out a warm invitation.

An angel Christmas tree ornament.

yards of silvery tinsel. Finally the last ornament was in place—except for the top.

Elizabeth gently unwrapped a lovely little fairy. The little figure was dressed in white tulle, and her tiny wings were a bit wilted from many years of use. She held a miniature wand in one hand. Dad carefully placed her at the very tip of the tree, and Mum switched off all the lights, leaving only the fireplace and the tree to illuminate the room.

"Oooh!" Elizabeth cried. "Isn't it beautiful?"

Mum agreed, "Grandmother still calls the Christmas tree our 'fairy tree,' and the lights 'fairy lights.'"

"I like that," Elizabeth crowed. "I think I'll call this one a fairy tree, too!"

"Here are the Christmas cards," Dad said, handing them out to the children. "We certainly have received a lot this year! You three can hang them up."

"And blow up the balloons!" Elizabeth puffed out her cheeks at Peter. "I can do them faster than you," she challenged.

In a short while, the living room looked as Christmassy as any shop window. Bunches of balloons and shimmering garlands hung from the ceiling, and long strings of Christmas cards added another cheerful touch. Red-berried holly and sprigs of evergreen adorned the fireplace mantel. The tree twinkled in the corner.

Mum collapsed on the sofa and put her feet up. Dad sank into a chair and lit his pipe. "I'd say we have all done a splendid job this time," he smiled. "We haven't forgotten anything, have we?"

"Yes, we have," Peter cried excitedly. "We haven't sent our letters to Father Christmas yet! Mine's all ready, too."

"So is mine," Tony chimed in. He was only five years old, and couldn't yet write well enough to compose such an important letter. He wanted to be sure that Father Christmas would be able to read it, so he had asked Peter—who was seven—to help.

Elizabeth rapidly scribbled her own list of desired presents on a scrap of paper. Kneeling before the fireplace, the youngsters tossed the letters onto the flames. Elizabeth's burned in a flash. So did Tony's. Peter's missed and lay at one side, smoldering a bit but not catching fire.

"You'll have to write another one," Elizabeth told him. "Father Christmas won't bring you what you asked unless the letter burns up. And it has to be a different list. You can't use the same one."

"Oh, all right," Peter grumbled. On the second try his letter burned to ashes instantly.

Curly-bearded Father Christmas greets a small friend at Harrods. Like Santa Claus in America, Father Christmas attracts thousands of children to British department stores every year.

Father Christmas is the British name for Santa Claus. Long ago in England the spirit of Yuletide revelry was symbolized by a merry figure, also called Father Christmas. He wore a wreath of mistletoe or holly upon his head, and his gown was sometimes red, but often green, white, or even brown. The Father Christmas of today, however, was imported from America a little more than a hundred years ago.

Santa Claus came to the New World with the Dutch settlers and, over the years, turned into the jovial, fat elf who delivers presents in a reindeer-drawn sleigh. The Santa figure which later began to appear in Britain was a mixture of America's merry sprite and the old Father Christmas. He is usually pictured as rather thin and tall, with a white beard, and wearing a long crimson robe with a hood or cap trimmed in white fur. At Christmastime many British department stores have a Father Christmas—some have a Santa Claus—who listens to children's wishes.

Tony and Peter went off to bed that night confident that their letters had reached their proper destination. Peter did wonder briefly how Father Christmas managed to read ashes—magic, he supposed.

A Wondrous Journey to Old England

The day before Christmas was a busy one for the Bushnells. There were presents still to be wrapped and placed beneath the tree, and last-minute baking to be done. In the afternoon Mum shooed everyone out, including Dad, to go ice-skating on a pond not far away.

"Just be back in time for tea," she called after them. When they came home, the tree was surrounded by even higher piles of gifts.

After supper that evening, each child was allowed to open one small present . . . a Christmas Eve custom in many British families. And they listened to the many bands of carolers being televised from all over London. Groups sang in great cathedrals, in crowded and lively pubs, outside the Tower of London, and even on barges on the River Thames.

Bundled up in coats and mittens, the children then went off to carol with their friends. Every year Peter and Elizabeth walked around the neighborhood, stopping to serenade waiting households. This was Tony's first chance to go with them.

Elizabeth held his hand as he bounced up and down with excitement. "Deck the hall with boughs of holly," he shouted happily.

"You're singing off-key," she hissed, then tried to drown him out by caroling even louder.

Some of the neighbors invited the youngsters in for hot drinks, and everyone gave them money. Tony wanted to keep his, but Elizabeth told him the money was being collected for charity. Just to be sure, she put the coins into her own pocket.

The youthful carolers finished their singing at the Bushnells, and then the other children ran home. Peter, Elizabeth, and Tony waved goodbye to their friends and went inside to warm themselves by the fire.

"Aren't you three planning to hang your stockings over the fireplace this year?" Dad teased.

Tony and Peter let out a whoop of joy, and raced from the room. They had been waiting for days for just this moment. Elizabeth followed more slowly. She could hear much whispering, shushing, and choked laughter in the boys' bedroom. The reason for their merriment became quickly evident when the pair raced back into the living room with two pillowcases instead of stockings!

"Clever," Dad commented dryly. "Now take them back and get your own stockings." Elizabeth wished she had thought of that—not that her greedy brothers had gotten away with it, though.

Members of the Blackheath Male Voice Choir sing carols to raise money for charity outside the Tower Hotel in London. Tower Bridge is in the background.

As soon as all three stockings were hung, empty and limp, Dad sat down in his big chair by the fire. Donning his glasses he opened a small, well-worn, red book. The boys sprawled on the floor at his feet, Mum and Elizabeth made themselves comfortable on the sofa.

"*A Christmas Carol*," Dad intoned solemnly. "By Charles Dickens. Chapter One. 'Marley was dead: to begin with.'"

Elizabeth breathed a deep sigh of contentment. Ever since she could remember, this was the best part of Christmas Eve, when Dad read aloud her favorite of all stories. She loved the classic tale about the ill-natured, stingy Ebenezer Scrooge and how the ghosts of Jacob Marley and the spirits of Christmas Past, Present, and Future appeared to him, in the end turning him into a kind and generous man.

Although she had heard the story often, she still enjoyed every word of it. The ghosts were always pleasurably scary; she could almost hear Marley's chains rattling. And when Tiny Tim Cratchit called out, "God bless us every one!" Elizabeth and Peter would both join in, echoing him.

" 'Merry Christmas! Out upon merry Christmas!' " Dad read in his snarliest voice. " 'What's Christmastime to you but a time for paying bills without money; a time for finding yourself a year older, and not an hour richer; a time for balancing your books and having every item in 'em through a round dozen of months presented dead against you? If I could work my will,' said Scrooge, indignantly, 'every idiot who goes about with "Merry Christmas" on his lips, should be boiled with his own pudding, and buried with a stake of holly through his heart. He should!' "

Elizabeth's head drooped. Her eyes closed. The warmth of the fire filled the room . . . her father's voice became dimmer. "I'm falling asleep," she thought . . . .

It's Christmas Eve, and the stockings are hung from the mantel. Will Father Christmas come down the chimney and fill them before morning? Of course he will!

21

Elizabeth's head drooped. Her eyes closed. The warmth of the fire filled the room… her father's voice became dimmer. "I'm falling asleep," she thought.

22

Or was she? Something odd had happened to the living room. Everything looked different. There was the Christmas tree, but now it was standing on a damask-covered table; real wax candles were burning on its branches. Where were Mum and Dad, and her brothers? Her own family seemed to have been replaced by another one. Near the tree, a young man and woman in old-fashioned clothes and six small children clapped their hands with glee at all the toys and dolls beneath it. Elizabeth was confused.

"You are a very fortunate child," a harsh voice grated in her ear. She jumped, startled by the old man who

An Edwardian Christmas tree. Mother lights a candle on the tree as little girls hug their new dolls.

stood beside her. He was tall, gaunt, and almost bald, with a wispy fringe of graying hair. His nose was sharp and long, and his thin mouth turned down at the edges.

"Who are *you?*" she whispered timidly.

"Ebenezer Scrooge, of course," the ominous figure snapped. "You know all about me—you should, you've been hearing my story every Christmas Eve of your life. You are privileged to have me as your escort back to the Christmases of the past . . . and who should know 'em better than I?" The old fellow uttered a rusty chuckle, and a twinkle flickered in his eye. It disappeared quickly, but Elizabeth saw it. Perhaps her odd companion wasn't quite as threatening as he had first seemed.

"Pay strict heed to what I say," Scrooge ordered. "I'll not repeat anything twice. By the way, none of the people we'll see can see us or hear us. And don't ask how that can be; if there is one thing I won't tolerate, it's a bothersome child."

He pointed a bony finger at the young woman across the room. "That is Queen Victoria. The man is her husband, Prince Albert. Those children belong to them, and we are in Windsor Castle. It is the year 1848, and the Christmas tree is Albert's gift to his family. He decorated it himself.

"Christmas trees aren't an English invention, you know," Scrooge went on. "They came from Germany. Albert was German, and probably homesick for his native land. A few years earlier, when he and Victoria were newly married, he decided to share his country's custom with his young English wife. But Victoria's Christmas trees weren't the first in England. A few others had already appeared, as far back as the beginning of the century. It wasn't until word spread about the Queen's trees, however, that the idea was taken up by ordinary people. Everyone wanted to imitate royalty's newfangled notion. Dickens called it, 'that pretty

A Victorian Christmas gathering. Children stare in awe at the Christmas tree and stacks of toys.

German toy.' Before many years had passed, Christmas trees could be found in households all over England.''

Elizabeth thought that Albert had done a fine job. An angel with outstretched wings perched at the top of the eight-foot fir, and exquisite little baskets and trays filled with candies and fruits hung from the branches. Fancy cakes and gilded gingerbread figures were also tied to the branches with colored ribbons. Elizabeth would have liked to look more closely at the toys . . . but Scrooge was speaking again.

"Queen Victoria ruled England from 1837 to 1901," he told her. "It was called the Victorian Era, and Charles Dickens lived then, too. Dickens loved Christmas. He did,

indeed! His descriptions of the Christmases of his day were so heartwarming and full of good-natured gaiety that they became a model for what people think of nowadays as a real British Christmas.''

Scrooge chuckled. "Men in tall hats and long mufflers caroling in the snow, roast geese or turkeys, plum puddings and steaming wassail bowls, holly and mistletoe, and ghost stories around the fire. Even though many of the customs Dickens wrote about began much earlier, that's a Dickensian Christmas! Watch now . . . you'll know this scene. It's Old Fezziwig's ball.''

Queen Victoria's family disappeared, and Elizabeth found herself in a room full of rollicking dancers. Men and women leaped about energetically, jigging to lively tunes played by a perspiring fiddler. Elizabeth's foot twitched; she wished she could join the revelers.

A large globe made of two hoops covered with holly and other greenery hung from the rafters. Ribbons, apples, and burning candles were attached to it, and a sprig of mistletoe dangled from it. Each time a couple danced beneath the globe, the man gave his partner a resounding kiss.

"Mistletoe." Scrooge muttered. "Bah! Don't approve of it. Inspires too much carrying on, in my opinion. That foolish object hanging there is called a 'kissing bough.' They were what people had before there were Christmas trees."

"Mistletoe was the Druids' sacred plant," Elizabeth said, wanting to show old Scrooge that she knew a few things, too. "They cut it down from the trees with a golden sickle. The Druids called it 'all-heal,' because they believed it could cure illnesses. Mistletoe protected you from witches, too."

"Hmph," Scrooge dismissed the information. "By the way, in the old days you'd never have seen mistletoe in a church. Christians forbade it because it was associated with those Druids you talk about, and their cruel pagan customs."

"It's not really very pretty, anyway," Elizabeth said meekly. "I like holly better."

"Holly was supposed to be hateful to witches, too," Scrooge snorted. "If you believe in such nonsense. Bringing holly and ivy into the house at Christmastime is a very ancient custom; even the Romans did it during their winter celebrations. The early Christians thought that holly resem-

The Royal Christmas tree, 1848. Queen Victoria, Prince Albert, and their children enjoy the glittering splendor of novel holiday decoration. Christmas trees were almost unknown in England before Victoria and Albert made them popular.

bled Christ's crown of thorns with its sharp-needled leaves and red berries like drops of blood. Ivy, on the other hand, was a symbol of Bacchus, the Roman god of wine. Long ago, holly was supposed to represent man and ivy represented woman. An old tradition was that if the Christmas holly was prickly, the master would rule the household for the coming year. If its leaves were smooth, then the mistress would rule."

"Ours is prickly," Elizabeth told him. "I guess that means that Dad will rule the house next year. I wonder if Mum knows about that tradition?" She laughed as one of the dancing couples almost crashed into the wall in their enthusiasm. "Queen Victoria's and Dickens' Christmas

A merry scene from A Christmas Carol by Charles Dickens—"Mr. Fezziwig's Ball."

26

Putting up holly and mistletoe, traditional activities on Christmas Eve, are shown in this wood engraving of 1855.

looks like fun. But what did people do at holiday time before then?"

"Ha!" Scrooge exclaimed. "England once celebrated Christmastide in a way that'll never be seen again. Everyone, high or low, enjoyed the merriest of holidays. Noble lords and ladies held open house, and the royal courts seethed with activity. There were Yule log ceremonies, jousting tournaments, spectacular pageants, and downright appalling displays of eating and drinking. Come along now—I'm going to show you what 'Merrie Olde England' was like."

They flew through the dark night, stars spinning in their galaxies, back and back, through centuries of time. Then they stopped suddenly, Elizabeth falling in a heap. She saw that she was sitting atop a scattering of rushes spread loosely over a stone floor—a cold stone floor. They were in a cavernous room—the ceiling loomed in darkness high above them. Glowing tapestries of enormous size

covered the walls, and there was an immense fireplace, the largest Elizabeth had ever seen.

Men and women dressed in gorgeous clothing made of rich, jewel-toned fabrics lounged at a long, wooden table at one end of the room. More guests roamed about the great hall, and servants ran to and fro bringing dish after dish of food or refilling goblets with ale and mead. Other servants carried in long iron spits with chunks of roasted meat. Dogs crouched here and there, always ready to snap up a tasty morsel of food tossed by one of the diners.

"Where are we?" Elizabeth asked. "And what year is it now?"

"We're in another castle—not Windsor. Never mind where it is,

They flew through the dark night, stars spinning in their galaxies, back and back, through centuries of time.

it's just somewhere in England. Castles all look alike to me, anyway," Scrooge said grouchily. "Blasted uncomfortable places they were, too. Bitterly cold, and damp. Look, the only light they had was from the fire and the candles—the poorer people had only bundles of rushes dipped in melted tallow fat to burn. A nasty, smoky way to light up a place it was," he sniffed. "As to the year, we are back in medieval times—the late Middle Ages. People began eating their dinner around noon then, and the meal went on for hours."

Elizabeth was fascinated by the dazzling spectacle. Minstrels strolled about entertaining the guests, and a jester cavorted gaily, his somersaults and cartwheels merrily jingling the bells on his cap. Jugglers tossed objects into the air, deftly caught them, and sent them soaring again.

An imposing gentleman in tights and rainbow-hued costume stalked about the hall, waving his hand in regal gestures. He seemed to be directing the proceedings. He wore a swooping hat that had long peacock feathers attached to the crown. A huge ruffled collar circled his neck, and an ermine-bordered cape fell from his shoulders. A small page boy followed him, holding up the end of the cape so it would not drag on the floor.

"Who is that?" Elizabeth asked, entranced.

"The Lord of Misrule," Scrooge informed her, glowering disapprovingly at the prancing figure. "A pagan practice. He acted as the leader, sort of a master of ceremonies, for the Christmas revels. The custom started in ancient Rome. Long before Christmas was even thought of, the Romans celebrated with a great feast in December, around the time of the winter solstice."

"That's when the shortest day of the year happens," Elizabeth said.

"Correct. The Romans called their festival the Saturnalia. Everything was turned topsy-turvy; the social order was totally reversed. Masters had to serve their slaves, men and women exchanged clothing, and many wore grotesque masks—even on the streets. In England, in the Middle Ages, that upside-down manner of celebrating popped up again . . . only now it was part of the Christmas festivities. Kings and nobles chose Lords of Misrule to reign over the entire holiday season, from Christmas to Twelfth Night."

Scrooge continued. "They were supposed to use all of their imagination—and large quantities of money —to think up games and amusing things to do. Everything had to be the exact opposite of normal everyday life, and continuous merriment

was the rule. Even kings and queens had to obey the Christmas Lords' orders, and they did! The custom continued for hundreds of years. Henry VII and Henry VIII both loved it. So did Queen Elizabeth I."

"My name's the same as hers," Elizabeth whispered. "She had red hair, though, and mine is brown." Scrooge scowled at the interruption.

"As I was about to say," he continued, "the rowdy, uproarious revelry caused by the Lord of Misrule was enormously popular. But it was severely frowned upon by the Church, and eventually the practice died out."

A new diversion now attracted Elizabeth's attention. Accompanied by a blaring fanfare of trumpets, a long procession entered the hall. First came a lady bearing a tray upon which reposed a whole peacock, its beak gilded and its tail feathers arranged in a fan of iridescent splendor. Then, the master cook marched in, surrounded by cheering onlookers. He proudly carried a silver tray bear-

In ages past in England, this resplendent gentleman, the Lord of Misrule, led the Christmas Revels. No matter how outrageous his demands, his rule was law during the holidays.

King Henry VII (1457-1509) kept Christmas at Westminster Hall. In this spectacular procession, the peacock and the boar's head make their way to the royal dinner table.

ing the head of a boar festively decorated with holly and rosemary sprigs, an orange in its mouth.

"Long ago," Scrooge told Elizabeth, "wild boar were common in England's thick forests. Dangerous beasts they were. There's a story about that. A student at Oxford University went off to study in the forest one day, and was attacked by a boar. To save himself the boy shoved his copy of Aristotle down the animal's throat and choked it to death. He brought the boar's head back to school, where it was duly roasted and eaten. The book was saved, too. Even today at Queen's College, Oxford, they celebrate the ancient Boar's Head Ceremony. The choir sings a traditional carol and the chief singer is presented with the orange from the boar's mouth."

Elizabeth was curious about the peacock. "Is it cooked?" she asked.

"Certainly," Scrooge snapped. "They skinned it, roasted it, and then put back the plumage. The nobility ate many strange things in those days—swans and wild cranes, porpoises, squirrels, and even whale. Roast beef, too, of course. Kings in olden times were quite accustomed to giving sumptuous banquets. Henry III ordered 600 oxen slaughtered for Christmas in 1252. King Richard II supposedly employed 2,000 cooks— but he had to. It's recorded that he fed 10,000 people every day, let alone at Christmas!

"And Henry VII offered his guests 120 dishes for one holiday feast. Even much later on, in 1770, there was a famous pie concocted for a baronet, Sir Henry Grey. It weighed 165 pounds and was nine feet around— stuffed with rabbits, ducks, geese, snipes, pigeons, blackbirds, and lots of other things. Had to be wheeled in on a special cart."

Elizabeth laughed. "It must have fed a crowd of hungry people. They don't have very good table manners, do they?" she added in a small voice, as she observed one guest wipe his greasy fingers on the fur of a dog lying at his feet. "But they're not using forks. Didn't they have any?"

"Forks came later," Scrooge explained. "And they were considered a luxury, at that."

"What is that porridge the lady in blue velvet is eating?" Elizabeth wanted to know.

"Plum pudding," Scrooge replied, peering in that direction.

"No, it's not. Plum pudding is round and hard. That's soupy."

"Don't argue with me," Scrooge growled. "Plum pudding was once just as you see it, a soupy dish made of mutton broth, dried fruit, and spices. They didn't boil it to make it hard until the 1600's—and, of course, the recipe was changed somewhat."

"I like the kind we have much better," Elizabeth told him. "Now what's happening?"

Through an arched doorway a band of servants had entered, dragging a

Masques and mummers' plays were favorite holiday entertainments in medieval England. The masquerade figures (below) *are from an illuminated manuscript of the period of King Edward III (1312-1377).*

gigantic oak log. As one end of the log was ceremoniously pushed into the fireplace, everyone in the vast hall broke into song.

"That is the Yule log," Scrooge said. "Scandinavian invaders brought the custom to England. The log was meant to burn all through the Christmas season, and the bits left over were kept to start the new log the following year. Most fireplaces aren't large enough to hold one any more, but the Yule log was once a yearly tradition in England."

"Didn't you mention jousting?" Elizabeth reminded him.

"I haven't forgotten," he said testily. "I may be old, but my mind hasn't gone yet. Christmas in the Middle Ages was one long boisterous round of gaiety. Besides the feasting, drinking, singing and dancing, people hunted, gambled, watched plays, and attended lavish tournaments. Knights were invited to come from all over the kingdom, even from Western Europe, to compete. One Christmas in the 1300's, Richard II held a tourney in which the pageantry and the tilting contests—dueling on horseback—lasted for almost two weeks. On the opening day, heralds and minstrels accompanied the courageous knights, and each challenger was led in by a young lady on horseback who held a silver chain attached to the knight's neck."

Elizabeth sighed wistfully. "That must have been exciting. My brothers would love to see a tournament. Me, too." But the room was beginning to blur; her head spun from all the noise and smoke, and strange smells.

Scrooge seemed to read her mind. "If you've seen enough of medieval Christmas, perhaps you'd be interested to know that there was a time when there wasn't any Christmas at all!"

"When was that?" she asked, astonished.

Old Ebenezer made a motion with his hand, and suddenly the two were looking down at a crowded street from atop a roof dotted with chimney pots. Shops were open, and people were going about their ordinary business. There were no Christmas decorations to be seen.

Bringing home the Yule log! This 1854 wood engraving portrays the excitement of the ancient custom of dragging a massive log from the woods to the hearth in an Old English country manor house. Once set aflame, the Yule log was supposed to burn throughout the Christmas season.

Christmas Day, 1873 — The Boar's Head Ceremony at Queen's College, Oxford University. The custom began hundreds of years ago, and is still carried on today.

"That is London," Scrooge pointed. "It's Christmas Day, 1649. A few years earlier, a group of people called Puritans, led by Oliver Cromwell, took over the country. The Puritans felt that the old ways of celebrating Christmas and other holidays had gotten out of hand, and finally Parliament abolished all religious festivities. Christmas was to be just another working day. The people rebelled. There were riots, and one mayor was beaten senseless by a mob. But the government held firm and, slowly, Christmas just about disappeared. On the surface, at least. Most people still celebrated it, but secretly — there was no more wild merrymaking. The Puritans even went so far as to ban mince pies."

Elizabeth giggled. "That's silly! Why did they do that?"

"Because at one time mince pies were baked in an oblong shape, to look like a manger. They often had a little image of the Christ Child on top. The Puritans thought that was too religious. So mince pies went into hiding, too. Later folks began to bake them again, but they were round, and much smaller."

Elizabeth frowned. How dreary it must have been if Christmas was just like every other day—no Father Christmas, no gifts, no Christmas dinner, no . . . . She felt frightened. What if Scrooge made a mistake and left her there? What if there were never to be another Christmas? She wished the dream would end . . . she wanted to go home.

Scrooge grumpily reassured her. "It turned out all right, you know. Christmas came back in 1660 when Charles II became king. But it was never quite the same . . . ." His voice trailed off.

"Elizabeth! Wake up!"

Elizabeth's eyes opened, and to her relief she saw that she was back in her own living room. Tony and Peter were playing with the cat, and Mum was coming in with hot chocolate and sweet biscuits. Dad smiled at Elizabeth.

"You fell asleep right in the middle of the story," he told her. "Mummy wouldn't let me wake you, though—and I guess you've heard the tale often enough, anyway."

"I'm sorry, Daddy," she smiled back, leaping up to hug him. "I do love that story, I love Ebenezer Scrooge, and I love Christmas! I'm so glad it's still here!"

Her parents looked at each other, puzzled. "Must have been dreaming," Dad decided. "I'd say it was time for bed, when you've finished your cocoa. The sooner you get to sleep the sooner it will be Christmas—and presents!"

"Elizabeth! Wake up!" Elizabeth's eyes opened, and to her relief she saw that she was back in her own living room.

33

Presents, Parties, and Pantomimes

Stockings come first on Christmas morning in Britain. Still heavy-eyed with sleep, Elizabeth and her brothers tumbled downstairs and raced for the fireplace. The once-empty stockings were now magically lumpy and misshapen—but not for long. There was a small Paddington Bear with yellow boots and slicker for Elizabeth, and bouncing little men on wooden sticks for the boys. Oranges, nuts, and candies were tucked into the stockings, too, and tiny puzzles to put together. Peter turned his stocking inside out to be sure he hadn't missed anything.

"Come to breakfast, everyone," Mum called. "After you finish, we have to get dressed for church."

Many people attend midnight services on Christmas Eve nowadays in England, but others go on Christmas morning. Massive Gothic cathedrals and small village churches resound with the joyous sound of bells and carols; altars, walls, and pews are decorated with branches of holly and fir. Rows of flickering candles light up the dark shadows, and Christmas trees add further touches of light and greenery.

The Bushnells attended services at a church not far from their house. To the children's delight, snow had fallen during the night. A fluffy frosting of white lay over the ground, glittering

in the pale, wintry sunlight. Elizabeth and her brothers kicked up little clouds of it as they walked along. Peter threw a snowball at Elizabeth, but Dad said no more of that—at least not until church was over.

Back home again, the boys claimed they were about to faint from hunger. Mum, smiling and flushed, soon announced that Christmas dinner was ready. A temptingly brown roast turkey, fat with stuffing, waited on a big platter to be carved. Surrounding it were little sausages, Brussels sprouts, and roast potatoes. A bowl of steaming giblet gravy sat close to the turkey. Dishes full of nuts and candies were scattered over the table, and there was a large Stilton cheese, too—for later.

"I think I like turkey better than peacock," Elizabeth said.

"Peacock!" Peter stared at her. "Who'd ever eat that?"

Elizabeth smiled at him. He'd never believe her if she told him. Her Christmas Eve dream was her secret, she decided.

The grand finale—the Christmas pudding—was carefully carried in by the two boys. Holly sprigs adorned it,

Children head homeward through the snow after Christmas morning service in an old Norman church in Kent.

and blue flames of burning brandy blazed over its rounded surface. Peter and Tony, showing off, pretended that they were being singed. Mum cut portions for everyone, and offered a pitcher of cream to pour over the pudding. Elizabeth and the boys bit cautiously into their servings, hoping to find the hidden coin. Tony was the lucky one.

All through dinner, the children had been eyeing gaily decorated tubes with twisted paper ends which were lying beside their plates. These were "crackers," an indispensable part of holiday celebrations in Britain.

Crackers are like birthday snappers in America, but much more ornate.

They come in a wide range of shiny colors, some have bits of holly, tiny silver bells, or paper flowers attached. The ends may be plain, or made of lacy paper. They are usually small, but one can find giant crackers, too, that are several feet long.

Tucked inside are silly paper hats and crowns, little toys, and strips of paper with funny riddles printed on them. They are not just for children . . . grown-ups also enjoy popping them, putting on the hats, and reading the riddles.

Now Dad nodded his head. "All right—everybody open the crackers!"

No holiday in Britain would be complete without Christmas crackers (right). These gaily decorated devices produce a loud bang when the ends are pulled, revealing toys, paper hats, and riddles inside. Sometimes it takes teamwork (below) to get to the hidden goodies.

A grandfather and his granddaughter open brightly wrapped gifts on Christmas morning beside the glowing fireplace.

The boys had a marvelous time, each tugging as hard as he could on his end of the tube until it went off with a bang. Then Elizabeth let Tony help pull hers. She read her riddle out loud.

" 'What do you call a train full of bubblegum?' "

"I give up," Mum laughed.

" 'A chew-chew train!' "

Everyone groaned. "My turn," yelled Tony. "Dad, you read mine for me."

"Here goes," Dad smiled. " 'What did one eye say to the other? There's something between us that smells!' "

"May we open our presents now?" pleaded Tony.

"Yes, please let's," Elizabeth and Peter begged. In short order, the living room was littered with torn wrapping paper and empty boxes. And gifts! The excited cat bounded from pile to pile, sniffing curiously, then leaping into the air to catch its tail or hiding under a crumpled piece of Christmas wrapping.

There were games and books and sweaters, a new pipe for Dad, an antique pewter bowl for Mum, and much, much more. Each of the boys received a toy wooden guardsman, with tall fur hat and red uniform. Elizabeth held up a pretty pink bathrobe for everyone to admire. Even the cat had a present—a green catnip mouse.

"Turn on the telly. It's time for the Queen's speech," Peter reminded them. Each Christmas, about 3 p.m., Queen Elizabeth II broadcasts a special holiday message to her subjects all over the world. Her grandfather, King George V, began the custom in 1932, and it is an occasion few Britishers would care to miss.

After the Queen's Christmas greeting, the family rushed off to a late afternoon party at a neighbor's house. While the adults chatted, the children played one of their favorite games, called Pass Around the Parcel. They sat in a circle and passed a wrapped parcel from child to child. One of the girls played a tune on the

A youngster eagerly unwraps a colorful Christmas present (right). Perhaps it contains a shiny toy wooden soldier (below) and his friends.

piano as the package went around, and the kids clapped their hands in time to the music—to keep from grabbing the parcel out of turn! Suddenly the music stopped, and the lucky child holding the parcel was the winner, getting to keep the present inside.

"When I was a boy," Dad reminisced, "we played a game called 'Snapdragon.' There was a large, shallow bowl full of flaming brandy with raisins in it. We'd try to grab as many raisins as possible with our fingers—and eat them."

"I remember doing that, too," Mum said. "I burned both my fingers and my tongue! Traditional or not, I think we'd better play something else."

Mrs. Nettleton, their hostess, spoke up. "Did you ever hear about 'Hot Cockles?'" she asked. "It's described in my new Christmas book. Listen: 'One person kneels or lies face downward in the center of the room and is blindfolded. The others in turn tap him on the shoulder, and he tries to guess their names. If he guesses correctly, that person takes his place.'"

"That doesn't sound very exciting," Peter sniffed.

"It could be," Mrs. Nettleton chuckled. "Here's a letter that was printed in a magazine in 1711: 'I am a Footman in a great Family and am in love with the House-maid. We were all at Hot-cockles last Night in the Hall these Holidays; when I lay down and was blinded, she pull'd off her shoe, and hit me with the Heel such a Rap, as almost broke my Head to Pieces. Pray, Sir, was this Love or Spite?'"

The children all howled with laughter. "I changed my mind," Peter grinned. "Let's play it."

"I don't think so," Dad told him. "The resulting wounds would be frightful to see. How about charades? And we'll all sing carols. Much safer. You young people can sing for us, and then we grown-ups will carol for you."

In a little while, Mr. Nettleton brought in a tray of items from the kitchen. "I'm going to make an old-fashioned wassail bowl," he announced.

British Christmas
partygoers sing carols
beneath hanging rows of
Christmas cards, a typical
holiday decoration.

He poured hot ale into a large
punch bowl, then added eggs, spices,
and sugar. He tossed in a few small
roasted apples, which made a hissing
noise as they bobbed about in the
steaming liquid. Elizabeth and the
other children watched with great
interest.

"The word *wassail* was originally a
Scandinavian term brought to England by the Vikings," Mr. Nettleton told them. "*Was hael* meant good
health. People toasted each other
with this drink. It's a kind of punch,
actually, and I'm using an authentic
old recipe. Sometimes it was also
called *lamb's wool*." He ladled out
cups for everyone—even a taste for
the youngsters. Elizabeth thought
it was delicious.

The Bushnells returned home soon
after that, tired out after the long day.
Everyone went to bed early that
night. It had been a good Christmas,
they all agreed.

The next day was also a holiday. It
was Boxing Day, which falls on the
first weekday after Christmas. Dad
explained the name to Tony.

"The day after Christmas is also
St. Stephen's Day," he said. "The
churches long ago had special boxes
for contributions at Christmas services. The boxes were opened on St.
Stephen's Day and the money inside
was given to the poor. People began
calling it Boxing Day sometime in
the Middle Ages. Later, the poor started to go around to wealthy households on that day to collect money.
Then it became the custom to give
presents of clothes, food, or money
to delivery boys and to such people
as the milkman, chimney sweep,
or postman on Boxing Day. Even
though the money was usually given
in an envelope by then, it was called
a 'Christmas Box.'"

"St. Stephen was the patron saint of
horses," Elizabeth put in. "I know
that because I love horses!"

In many parts of Britain, a fox hunt is a traditional Boxing Day event. Although fox hunts are often met with some protest for their violent premise, many who attend them do so to witness their grand pageantry. Elegant ladies and gentlemen wearing black jackets or bright hunting pink—which is actually red—sit astride polished, sleek horses. Proud youngsters ride fat ponies. A pack of shiny brown and white hounds mill about, baying excitedly and straining at their leashes. Stirrup cups, the customary farewell drinks, are passed up to the riders, and then—they are off!

Boxing Day is also the big day for football (soccer) games in Britain. Motor car races are popular, too.

Peter was playing in his school's football match that afternoon, and the rest of the family went along to watch. Peter's team won, and Tony, who hoped he would be big enough to play next year, was overjoyed.

After Boxing Day, the most important Christmastime event was the annual visit to the pantomime. It's a typically British affair, the Christmas pantomime—at least the way they present it. To Americans, pantomime means acting with the body, without words. In Britain, it's a lot more than that, and great fun for children and adults alike.

In the large cities, especially London, top television and stage personalities star in pantomimes. These are splendidly lavish extravaganzas costing many thousands of dollars to produce. Traditionally, there is a "Dame" who is played by a man. The "Principal Boy" used to be played by a girl wearing tights to show off her pretty legs. Nowadays, this is not considered as daring as it once was, so the role may be acted by either male or female.

At a fox hunt, a traditional Boxing Day event, smartly dressed riders and a hallooing pack of hounds await the signal to set off on their rousing chase through the countryside.

The stories are spoofs of old fairy tales, with songs, silly jokes, and comments on current events added. *Cinderella*, *Puss in Boots*, *Jack and the Beanstalk*, and similar tales have all been favorite pantomimes for years. In recent seasons, new ones have been added, such as *Hans Christian Andersen* and *Peter Pan.*

It's not known for sure how the British style of pantomime began, but it probably goes back to the *commedia dell'arte*, a type of comedy that developed in Italy in the 1500's in which actors made up dialogue as they went along. English pantomime dates from the early 1700's. John Rich, owner, actor, and manager of Lincoln's Inn Fields Theatre in London, produced one of the first, in 1717. Like all the pantomimes to follow, the performance included a wondrous "transformation" in which huts and cottages were changed into palaces, and just about everything on stage—even the actors—seemed to become something else. It was so well received that Rich eventually presented and performed in pantomimes at three theaters—Covent Garden, Drury Lane, and his own—for the next 43 years.

The Bushnells went to see *Aladdin.* Elizabeth thought the oriental costumes and scenery, all Chinese reds and golds, were just super. She and the boys—and their parents—cheered for Aladdin, and whenever the evil magician appeared, they hissed. The lively interaction between the players and the audience was exciting for everyone. Characters on stage called out to the kids in the theater, and the children yelled right back!

Pantomime, a typically British form of theater, is a favorite family diversion at Christmastime. Shown is a scene from Aladdin.

The rest of the holiday season raced by all too fast. On New Year's Day, the Bushnells were invited to tea by Mrs. Bushnell's parents, who lived not far away. Tony, Peter, and Elizabeth had been looking forward to that annual get-together. They enjoyed visiting their grandparents, and seeing some of their aunts, uncles, and cousins, too.

Around four o'clock Grandmother served a huge tea—lots of little sandwiches and hot, buttery scones, and another traditional holiday treat, the Christmas cake. Rich and dark with fruit and nuts, covered with a layer of marzipan and then thickly frosted, the cake was a roaring success. There were also small, tart-sized mince pies with brandy butter. Peter began piling up a precariously tilting stack of pies.

Another scene from Aladdin, *one of the many popular pantomimes put on during the Christmas season in England.*

"Just what do you think you're doing?" Dad inquired.

"My teacher said it used to be the custom to eat one mince pie on each of the twelve days of Christmas," Peter explained, looking innocent. "That way you'd have good luck for all the months of the year."

The fearsome Captain Hook matches wits with Peter in this traditional Christmas season production of Peter Pan, *at the London Casino Theatre. J. M. Barrie's classic play has been shown in London almost every Christmas since it was first produced in 1904.*

"Very interesting," Mum laughed. "But you did say one a day, not all 12 at once. And anyway, there just aren't enough pies for all of us to do that. So — put them back."

Outside, darkness had fallen; Grandfather built up the fire and told scary ghost stories, the children gathered in a cluster at his feet. Grandmother brought out still more goodies to eat, and handed everyone a present.

"It's the old way," she smiled. "People used to give gifts at New Year's, not Christmas. Queen Elizabeth I used to receive so many presents that she hardly needed any new clothes for a year! Her ladies-in-waiting, the royal physician, even the master cook all gave her something — gowns, jewelry, candy. She loved sweets, especially marzipan molded into all kinds of shapes — even a chessboard, one year."

"Her subjects didn't always give her those presents voluntarily," Grandfather added. "Like most of the other sovereigns before her, she 'requested' them. No one was foolish enough to refuse. I don't know if he asked for it or not, but I recall reading that Henry III once received a rather un-

usual gift from the King of France — a live elephant!"

Tony looked longingly at his father, who laughed.

"No, you may not have an elephant. And it's time we all went home."

Twelfth Night, January 5, marks the end of the Christmas season in Britain. Elizabeth reminded her family that the moment had come to remove the Christmas decorations.

"Unless we do," she warned them solemnly, "we'll have bad luck, and goblins might get in and make a mess."

"I'd like to see a goblin," Peter muttered darkly. "I'd catch him and make him show me his pot of gold."

"Goblins don't have pots of gold," Elizabeth informed him. "You're thinking of leprechauns." She and her mother began to take down the holly and the Christmas cards. Peter and Tony popped all the balloons they could reach, and Dad wrapped up the ornaments in tissue paper. Elizabeth spotted a silver ball that had fallen behind the tree. She crawled under the now barren branches to retrieve it from the cat, which was batting it with its paws. Lying beside the ornament was a small package with a red bow on it.

"I found something!" she cried. "It's another present. And it's for me!"

"Goodness, that's right," her mother said. "That's your New Year's gift from Grandmother. You forgot to open it, so I brought it home and put it under the tree."

Tearing off the paper, Elizabeth looked at the present with astonishment. It was a new copy of Dickens' *A Christmas Carol.* Opening it to the flyleaf, she read: "To Elizabeth. Your very own Christmas story." It was signed "Ebenezer Scrooge." But she recognized the handwriting . . . it was Grandmother's. Elizabeth smiled happily, then laughed out loud.

"What's so funny?" the boys wanted to know.

"Oh, nothing," she said, giggling. "It's just that Ebenezer Scrooge happens to be a personal friend of mine!"

Dad ruffled her hair as Peter hooted derisively. Only Elizabeth heard the rumbling chuckle that floated through the air . . . and the creaky old voice which uttered two words.

"Bah! Humbug!"

Tearing off the paper, Elizabeth looked at the present with astonishment. It was a brand new copy of Dickens' *A Christmas Carol.* . . . It was signed "Ebenezer Scrooge."

The Welsh Mari Lwyd *snaps its fearsome jaws. A kind of hobbyhorse, the Mari Lwyd prances in a procession of mummers and musicians, stopping at houses along the way.*

Christmas
Customs
Around
the Land

Christmas is a time for tradition, and a host of strange and picturesque customs of the past are still observed faithfully in Britain each year. Some are very old, dating back to pagan times or the Middle Ages. Others have come into being in more recent centuries; many are traceable to the various conquerors who came from other lands. The people who live in England, Scotland, and Wales each have their own unique ways of observing the Christmas season, and each regional custom adds another element to the merry mixture of celebrations that is British Christmas.

Play-acting has been part of English Christmastime entertainment for hundreds of years. Mystery plays, portraying episodes in the life of Christ, were popular in the Middle Ages. There were miracle plays, too, religious dramas about saints and martyrs. In the royal courts, *masques* were once a favorite holiday fare. They were pageantlike theatricals in verse, in which the performers dressed in elaborate costumes and masks. Kings and queens often took roles themselves, and in the 1600's several masques were written especially for the royal family by Ben Jonson, the famous dramatist. By the 1700's, masques had disappeared, replaced by the pantomime.

Another form of ancient drama still exists today in England—the mummers' play. Like the miracle and mystery plays, it was originally a folk drama, but its roots were more pagan than religious. The mummers' play celebrates the return of spring once again after the long winter, or the coming back to life after death.

Customarily, only men perform the roles. They wear fanciful costumes and either wear masks or blacken their faces. Early mummers often wore grotesque animal masks on their heads; some dressed in straw costumes or were covered with colored strips of paper. In most versions of the play, and there are many, the players are led in by Father Christmas, who also sets the scenes. The names of the characters and number of players vary widely, but certain basic types are always present.

The hero, St. George, kills a fierce dragon, and fights a battle with an evil Turkish knight. A sword dance is often part of the play, ending with the mock death of St. George. A quack doctor brings the hero back to life, and one or two comical fellows collect money from the audience. The play is all in rhyme, and performed with great gusto, with songs and dances mixed in.

Sometimes mummers' plays include a character dressed up like a hobbyhorse. In some regions the hobbyhorse goes about with its own procession of mummers, and is called the Hodening Horse. The head is handcarved from wood and fixed to a pole. It has two dug-out eyes, and a huge jaw with large teeth which are made to clack and snap by pulling a string. Ribbons, rosettes, and jingling bells are added for decoration. Covered with a cloth or blanket the rider romps about astride the pole in bent-over position so that he resembles a real horse. A lighted candle may be placed in the hollow of the head, causing the mouth to glow like a fiery furnace — a fearsome sight, especially when seen peering into a window at night!

Wales has a similar custom called Mari Lwyd. The leading mummer wears the ribbon-bedecked skeleton of a horse's head. The bizarrely costumed players visit previously selected houses and go through a kind of battle of wits with the householders. They bang loudly on the door with a stick and sing out impromptu verses; the people inside must reply with more made-up verse. If the horse and his group can outwit the host, they are invited in for cakes and cider.

There's a legend from the Middle Ages that says the Glastonbury Thorn will blossom whenever a member of the royal family visits Glastonbury, in Somerset. The Vicar plucks off a bud and presents it in a silver box to the royal visitor. The tale of the magical Thorn began many centuries ago, when St. Joseph of Arimathea was said to have come to England to preach the Gospel. He journeyed to Glastonbury's Wearyall Hill, where, on Christmas Eve, he thrust his hawthorn staff into the ground.

The staff took root and grew, and every year it blossomed at midnight on December 24. The old hawthorn was destroyed by soldiers during the Puritan era, but cuttings from it had already been planted elsewhere. One such descendant grows in the ruins of Glastonbury Abbey. In 1752, the calendar was changed in England. To do this, the government had to eliminate 11 days. The people didn't like it one bit. The holidays were now all out of kilter, and they thought that they had been robbed, somehow, of those missing days.

Hoden horses and their gaily costumed attendants cavort at a celebration in Smarden, Kent.

Atop the mounting stone by the village church the "fool" recites the ancient legend of the Haxey Hood Game *at Haxey, Humberside.*

Traditionally, the legendary Glastonbury Thorn (below) blooms each year during the Christmas season. It is said to be the descendant of the hawthorn that grew from the staff of St. Joseph of Arimathea, planted centuries ago at Glastonbury.

GLASTONBURY THORN.

That year, and for several years after, the Glastonbury Thorn was watched with great interest—would it flower on the old Christmas Eve, or the new, on what had been January 5? Supposedly, it bloomed on the old more often than not, confirming the people's belief that the government had wickedly interfered with the true date of Christ's birth. The Glastonbury Thorn still blooms pretty much on schedule. The truth of the matter is that the Thorn is a flowering type which normally blooms twice a year, and one of those is at Christmastide.

One Sunday in the early 1200's, it is said, Lady de Mowbray was out riding and her hood blew off. Twelve *boggans* (farmworkers) chased and recovered it. The lady was so impressed by their gallant efforts that she willed a piece of land to the village for as long as the inhabitants would reenact the event once a year. The town of Haxey, Humberside, in Lincolnshire, has kept that promise. The gigantic rough-and-tumble called the Haxey Hood Game takes place there every January 6.

Costumed boggans, the "Lord," and a "fool" start off with lunch and songs at one local pub, followed by more singing at the other pub. Orig-

49

inally, the people then "smoked"
the fool by standing him atop a pile
of damp paper and straw, and setting
it afire. However, this proved too
dangerous and was stopped.

Nowadays the group heads for a
field, where 12 sack hoods are thrown
up and the children try to capture
them from the boggans. Later, a much
larger leather hood is tossed up and a
mad tug-of-war called the *sway* forms
around it. Teams of men, some from
neighboring villages, push and shove
for several hours, until the hood is
finally and victoriously carried to one
of the pubs. Drinks are on the house,
and the hood remains in that pub
until the following year. Interested
observers report that, to date, no one
has been seriously injured.

The Goathland Plough Stots of
North Yorkshire also perform an-
nually in early January. *Stot* meant
a bullock in old English, but somewhere along the way the word came
to apply to the young men who drag
a plow in the procession. A "Lord"
and "Lady" lead off, followed by
"Toms," men dressed in costumes.
Sword dancers, musicians, and the

plow stots come behind. Wherever
the procession stops, the sword dancers go through their elegant, intricate routine, and the Toms cavort
with amusing antics. A collection
is taken up by "Madgy-pegs," men
dressed in women's clothes, some
of whom are on stilts to reach spectators in upper-story windows.

Although Christmas and its customs were in disfavor for only a short
time in England, Scotland ignored
the holiday far longer. It has only
been in recent years that the Scots
observed December 25 as a special
day at all. But New Year's Eve — that
is something else again! It's called
Hogmanay, and is celebrated with
great enthusiasm.

Up Helly Aa, *the "end of the year" celebration in the Shetlands, commemorates the days of the Norse invaders. Torch-bearing participants gather around a dragon-prowed Viking galley in the town square. Then they throw their torches into the hull and set it aflame.*

Revelers throng the streets of cities and towns to await the tolling of the bells that announce midnight and the New Year. Traditionally, the head of a household opens the door wide at that moment, to let out the Old Year and allow the New Year to enter.

At midnight, also, the custom of "first-footing" commences. Superstition has it that the first person to cross the threshold after the New Year has begun must be a dark-haired man. It is thought that the reason for this goes back to the days of the Viking invaders, who were usually blond or red-haired. No sensible householder would let one of those come through the door!

Also considered to be bad luck first-footers are the lame, flat-footed persons, persons blind in one eye, those with eyebrows meeting over their noses, or anyone of low moral character. Women bring the worst luck of all. Because one cannot trust to chance that the right sort of person will enter first, dark-haired male relatives are sometimes called upon to perform the ritual. Groups of

young men often band together and go from house to house, first-footing their friends. A lump of coal, a piece of cake, and a pinch of salt are traditional first-footers' gifts to their hosts. In return, they receive a welcoming New Year's drink.

Up Helly Aa in the Shetlands is another reminder that Norsemen once ruled Scotland. It takes place on the last Tuesday in January, and reenacts the Nordic celebration of the triumph of the sun over the darkness of winter. Hundreds of men in Viking dress and horned helmets march beside a 30-foot Viking galley in a torchlit procession ending at the town square. Gathering around the dragon-prowed ship, the men throw their torches into its hull. Singing a rousing traditional song, they and the fascinated onlookers watch it burn, flames shooting dramatically up into the dark night sky.

Burning the Clavie *(tar-barrel) takes place on Old New Year's Eve (January 11) in Burghead, Grampian, a fishing village on the southern shore of the Moray Firth.*

"Burning out the old year" is the basis for several other ancient customs. The Tar-Barrel Parade sets forth every December 31 in Allendale, in northern England. Men called "guisers," wearing disguises, carry "tar-kits," old beer or fish barrels cut in half and filled with wood shavings covered with paraffin. The barrels are heavy, weighing 30 to 40 pounds each. Just before midnight, the procession, including a band, marches around the town and ends up at the market place. The guisers throw the tar barrels onto a huge bonfire there and sing "Auld Lang Syne" as midnight strikes.

Burning the Clavie is a similar New Year's Eve ritual in Burghead, in Scotland. The people there use only one specially prepared barrel, the clavie. They pour tar over bits of wood in the clavie and set it afire with burning peat. The carrier thrusts his head through a hole in the barrel and staggers off with it balanced on his head and shoulders. He changes off at various points with other carriers, and bits of the clavie are handed out to the crowd for good luck. The burning tar often drips down onto the carrier—a very uncomfortable sensation, undoubtedly. The procession ends on a hill where the clavie is smashed with a hatchet.

Twelfth Night—January 5—was once surrounded by customs and legends. A Twelfth Night Cake was always baked, with a bean and a pea inside. Whoever found the bean was named King of the Revels; the pea proclaimed the Queen. A Twelfth Night Cake is still served in the green room of Drury Lane Theatre in Lon-

don. Attendants wearing powdered wigs and 18th-century livery carry in the cake, courtesy of Robert Baddeley, a chef turned actor. He died in 1794, leaving 100 pounds sterling to be invested with the interest to be used for cake and wine for the actors to share each year in his memory.

Until just recently, the apple farmers of Carhampton, in Somerset, wassailed their apple trees on Old Twelfth Night (January 17) each year. Carrying guns, lanterns, and a pail of cider, they would gather around a chosen tree. They would place a piece of toast soaked in cider in the fork of the tree for the birds and pour more cider around the tree's roots. The men would then fire their guns into the branches, and toast the tree with mugs of cider and an ancient wassail song: "Here's to Thee, Old Apple Tree."

"Guisers" carry burning "tar-kits" on their heads in the New Year's Eve Tar-Barrel Parade in Allendale, Northumberland.

The first Christmas card,
designed by John Calcott
Horsley in 1843, was
lithographed on stiff card-
board and hand-colored.
The center panel shows a
family party drinking a
toast; side panels show gifts
of food and clothing being
given to the poor.

Christmas Greetings from Britain

In 1843, John Calcott Horsley designed a hand-colored, printed Christmas greeting card. It sold for a shilling in a shop on Bond Street in London. Only about 1,000 copies were sold—a shilling was considered a fairly steep price in those days, especially for a novelty. Today, the Christmas card industry has grown into a giant, and each year at holiday time the post office reels under the blizzard of seasonal greetings.

There are undoubtedly those who consider the whole thing a nuisance. But when that first card arrives in the mail, it all suddenly seems worthwhile. It's a joyful sign that the Christmas season has truly begun.

Sending Christmas and New Year greetings was not unknown in Britain before the 1840's. People sent their friends holiday letters, or small cards about the size of our business cards, with the sender's name and perhaps "Christmas" written in by hand. And schoolchildren laboriously copied out messages called "Christmas pieces" on colored sheets of paper with decorated borders and took them home at the end of winter term to show their parents how much their penmanship had improved.

Horsley designed his innovative creation for Henry Cole, who later became Sir Henry Cole, the first director of London's Victoria and Albert Museum. Too busy that year to write his usual Christmas letters, Cole suggested the idea of a special, illustrated holiday card to Horsley, an eminent artist.

A great deal of controversy later arose as to whether Horsley's Christmas card was actually the first. A young artist, William Maw Egley, had also designed a Christmas card about the same time. The date on it appeared to be either 1842 or 1848. After much close scrutiny, most sources decided that Egley's card must have appeared in 1848.

In the next few years, cheaper printing techniques made Christmas cards more affordable to the general public. Then, a special half-penny stamp for postcards and unsealed envelopes was introduced in 1870, making the practice even more economical. Ten

Along with other costumed children, a young chef points a dancing toe in a merry Christmas celebration. The card was printed by Marcus Ward and Co. of London in the late 1800's.

A HAPPY CHRISTMAS

FAR BEST OF ALL THE CHRISTMAS FUN, THE MERRY DANCE WHEN DINNER'S DONE

Red-berried holly branches twine about a curly-haired angel on this Christmas card, printed in the late 1800's.

Christmas Blessings be yours

The cheery red-breasted robin has long been a Christmas symbol in Britain.

The Wishing Bone.

Wishing you a happy Christmas.

years later, the Post Office first issued that familiar appeal: "Post Early for Christmas."

Also in 1880, Great Britain began a nationwide Christmas card design competition. This event attracted much publicity, and the Christmas card industry began to develop. Famous artists contributed their talents, and England's poet laureate, Alfred Lord Tennyson, was invited to write some verses for cards. He refused, regretfully, because of age and ill health.

The Christmas cards of the late 1800's would astonish most people today with their variety and ingenuity. It was the romantic Victorian era, and many of the early cards resembled today's Valentines. Purely Christmas motifs soon came into their own—but many of the cards were lacy-edged and flowery.

Typical scenes on the cards of the times included snowy country views bordered by designs of holly and ivy, merry drawings of happy people eating and drinking, and sentimental sketches of charitable acts and pathetic orphans. Snowflakes, carolers, skaters on frozen ponds, fireside gatherings and stage coaches, cherubs and children—even soldiers and comic animals—adorned the cards.

The red-breasted robin was one of the most popular Christmas card

symbols. Postmen, because of their red uniforms, were then known as "robin postmen." But the robin had long been a British favorite, representing a cheery, bright contrast to winter's bleakness. One early series of cards, however, offered a grimmer sight—dead robins. This melancholy theme may have come from the ancient custom of killing a wren or robin at Christmastime—or perhaps a subtle protest against such killings.

Victorian Christmas cards came in every conceivable shape, too: crescents and stars, fold-out fans, and as elaborate boxes or purses. They were printed on velvet, plush, satin, and lace; they were painted on porcelain; they were jeweled, beaded and frosted, tasseled and fringed; and many had intricate cutout designs which stood up when the card was opened. One was in the form of a bullfinch, which flapped its wings and whistled when pressed.

The cards were reproduced by chromolithography, which required 10 or 12 engravings to print a single card. The result was an imaginative piece of artful perfection which would be a collector's item today.

Over the years, Christmas cards have become more standardized and much more commercial, but their popularity has never slackened. Sentiment goes hand-in-hand with Christmas; cheerful holiday scenes are welcome forerunners of the season. And the old, timeless message of "peace, good will toward men," never goes out of style.

Stagecoaches were another favorite Christmas card motif in the 1800's. The message on this one is a quote from Charles Dickens.

Early Victorian Christmas cards, with lacy borders and winsome cherubs, often resembled Valentines (below).

The dancers in this card (above) produced in 1872, move when the tab at the bottom of the card is pulled.

*Dressed in Dickensian
attire typical of the late
1800's, the Blackheath Male
Voice Choir welcomes the
Christmas season in
London. An amateur group
made up of businessmen,
policemen, and others, they
raise funds for charity by
singing in pubs, hotels,
clubs, and restaurants.*

The Joyous Sounds of Christmas

Mighty cathedral bells ring out in golden peals! Small handbells chime their clear, bright notes, and singers young and old carol the ancient Yuletide songs of praise and joy. Christmas in Britain is ushered in on a wave of jubilant sound!

Caroling is one of the oldest British Christmas customs, going back to the Middle Ages. Beggars at Christmastime would wander the streets of a town, singing in return for money, food, or drink. Carols were often sung between the acts of medieval mystery plays—the lovely *Coventry Carol* is one of these. Minstrels went from castle to castle singing Christmas songs, and in later years every town had its own band of Waits.

Waits were originally watchmen who patrolled the streets of the old walled cities. They would sing out the hours of the night, or blow notes or tunes on musical instruments. Eventually the term was applied to groups of musicians that sang and played for various civic social affairs. During the Christmas season they would make nightly rounds of the town, serenading the inhabitants. Not everyone enjoyed their services, however. Some citizens complained bitterly of being rudely awakened from a sound sleep as the Waits caroled beneath their windows.

Today it seems that virtually everyone in Britain goes a-caroling at Christmas. Schools, civic groups, and organizations of all sorts present programs of carols, many of them aimed at collecting money for charity. Carolers gather in homes, on street corners, and in every church. And caroling goes on at that pace throughout the Christmas holidays, not just on Christmas Eve.

In London, Christmas music is presented almost daily in the cathedrals and concert halls. Midnight services at Westminster Abbey and St. Paul's on Christmas Eve are always crowded with people. At King's College Chapel, Cambridge, the beautiful Festival of Nine Lessons and Carols is celebrated every Christmas Eve afternoon. The chapel is illuminated only by the flickering light of countless candles. The choir

The lovely Festival of Nine Lessons and Carols is held each year on Christmas Eve afternoon at King's College Chapel, Cambridge University.

enters in procession, each singer carrying a lighted candle. During the service, readings from scripture alternate with the singing of nine traditional carols.

In Greek and Roman days, a carol was a ring dance, an important part of all festivals. Words were later added, and eventually carols came to be associated only with the celebration of Christmas. "The Holly and the Ivy" and the Wassail song probably date back to the Middle Ages. "The Boar's Head Carol" and "Yule Log Carol," too, have been sung since ancient times in England.

Britain today has a host of favorite carols, including "The Twelve Days of Christmas," "Hark! The Herald Angels Sing," "Good King Wenceslas," "God Rest You Merry, Gentlemen," and "I Saw Three Ships Come Sailing In." "Once in Royal David's City" is sung at the start of the Festival of Nine Lessons and Carols at Cambridge. The words were written by Mrs. Cecil Frances Alexander, wife of the Bishop of Derry. She wrote

hundreds of hymns, and this one was composed for her godchildren, to tell them the story of Jesus' birth in simple verse. A popular carol of Victorian days, still occasionally sung today, is "In the Bleak Mid-Winter," the lyrics written by the famous English poet, Christina Rosetti.

Like folk tales, carols were passed down from generation to generation for centuries. Few were printed until the 1800's, although a collection called a *Sette of Carols* was published about 1521. Carols were severely discouraged during the Puritan period in England, and they almost disappeared for 200 years. Only the long memories of country folk preserved them.

Wales, especially, kept the tradition alive. The Welsh are a nation of singers and poets, holding national song and literary competitions called *eisteddfods*. The largest of these is held in August, and draws enormous crowds every year. At Christmastime, others are held throughout the country, just for caroling. Townsfolk gather in the market place, where trained choirs lead them in singing. New carols are composed each year for the Yuletide contests, and the winning songs are added to the repertoire of Christmas music.

Music is an integral part of Welsh life, especially at Christmas. The Welsh poet Dylan Thomas, in *A Child's Christmas in Wales*, wrote: "Always on Christmas night there was music. . . . Looking through my bedroom window, out into the moonlight and the unending smoke-colored snow, I could see the lights in the windows of all the other houses on our hill and hear the music rising from them up the long, steadily falling night. . . ."

Plygain (Crowing of the Cock), the Christmas dawn service once held everywhere in Wales, was often accompanied by as many as 15 carols.

The overflowing church would be ablaze with candles as the singers caroled forth in solos, duets, trios, and full choruses. According to one account from the 1800's, the rector might also include a sermon, but he made sure to keep it short, because the congregation became restless between carols!

Britain is sometimes called "The Ringing Isle," and the ancient art of *campanology* (bell-ringing) is still widely practiced. In early times, bells were considered almost human, and were given the names of saints, and baptized. Sometimes, too, bells were named after their donors. At Christmas, bells throughout the land ring out the complicated sequences, called changes, over country fields and city rooftops. On Christmas Eve afternoon in London, the bells of St. Paul's Cathedral ring in the coming of Christmas with a clamoring peal which lasts for half an hour. Shortly

Youthful choristers sing carols beside a Christmas crib at Salisbury Cathedral.

Mighty bells in church belfries throughout Britain ring to greet the coming of Christmas.

(facing page)
This reconstruction of a street scene from the past in the Castle Museum in York shows carol singers gathered around a lamppost.

after it begins, the bells of Westminster Abbey join in.

At Crowland, in Lincolnshire, the choir sings carols from the ancient battlements of the Abbey on Christmas Eve. When the carols end, bell ringers in the belfry take over, sending out their own Christmas message. Handbell ringers tour villages in many parishes during the weeks before Christmas, playing their traditional music as they go. The handbells of Standon, Hertfordshire, have belonged to the village since 1870.

A custom called "Tolling the Devil's Knell" has been practiced for 700 years at Dewsbury, in Yorkshire. On Christmas Eve bell ringers toll "Black Tom," the tenor bell of the parish church. Thomas de Sothill gave the bell to the church as a token of remorse for having murdered a servant. He declared that it must sound a *knell* (announcement of death) every Christmas from that time forward. The ceremony proclaims an old belief that the Devil died at the birth of Christ. One ring is tolled for every year since Jesus was born, the final ring timed to strike exactly at midnight.

The joyful sounds of British Christmas have never been described more aptly than in a passage from *A Christmas Carol,* by Charles Dickens. The newly-reformed Scrooge has awakened on Christmas morning "merry as a schoolboy" at having been given a second chance for happiness:

"He was checked in his transports by the churches ringing out the lustiest peals he had ever heard. Clash, clang, hammer; ding, dong, bell. Bell, dong, ding; hammer, clang, clash! Oh, glorious, glorious!

"Running to the window, he opened it, and put out his head. No fog, no mist; clear, bright, jovial, stirring, cold; cold, piping for the blood to dance to; Golden sunlight; Heavenly sky; sweet fresh air; merry bells. Oh, glorious. Glorious! . . . Christmas Day!"

A British
Christmas Sampler

Carols of Good Tidings

Coventry Carol

Robert Croo, 1543

English Melody, 1591

When Christ was Born of Mary Free

Harleian Manuscript, 1456

16th Century English [WE]

Allegretto moderato

1. When Chist was born of Ma-ry free, In Beth-le-hem that fair ci-ty,
2. The King is come to save man-kind, As in the scrip-ture truths we find,
3. Then, dear-est Lord, for Thy great grace, Grant us in bliss to see Thy face,

An-gels sang there with mirth and glee:
There-fore this song we have in mind,
That we may sing to Thy so-lace,

"In ex-cel-sis glo-ri-a."

REFRAIN

In ex-cel-sis glo-ri-a, In ex-cel-sis glo-ri-a,

In ex-cel-sis glo-ri-a, In ex-cel-sis glo-ri-a.

In ex-cel-sis glo-ri-a, In ex-cel-sis glo-ri-a.

The Boar's Head Carol

17th Century English

18th Century English Carol [WE]

1. The boar's head in hand bear I, Be-decked with bays and rose-ma-ry; And I
2. The boar's head as I un-der-stand is the fin-est dish in all the land, When
3. Our stew-ard hath pro-vid-ed this In hon-or of the King of Bliss, Which

pray you, my mas-ters, be mer-ry, Quot es-tis in con-vi-vi-o, [1]
thus be-decked with a gay gar-land, Let us ser-vi-re can-ti-co. [2]
on this day to be serv-ed is, In Re-gi-nen-si a-tri-o. [3]

REFRAIN

Ca-put a-pri de-fe-ro, Red-dens lau-des Do-mi-no. [4]

[1]*You who are at this feast*
[2]*Serve by singing*
[3]*In the royal hall*
[4]*The boar's head I bear,*
Giving praises to the Lord.

From *The International Book of Christmas Carols* by Walter Ehret and George K. Evans © 1963 by PRENTICE-HALL, INC., Englewood Cliffs, New Jersey. Reprinted by permission.

Deck the Hall with Boughs of Holly

Traditional Welsh

Old Welsh Carol

Allegro

1. Deck the hall with boughs of hol-ly,
2. See the blaz-ing Yule be-fore us,
3. Fast a-way the old year pass-es,

Fa la la la la, la la la la,

'Tis the sea-son to be jol-ly,
Strike the harp and join the cho-rus,
Hail the new, ye lads and lass-es,

Fa la la la la, la la la la.

Away in a Manger

Anonymous

J.R. Murray, 1877 [WE]

Andante

1. A - way in a man - ger, no crib for a bed, The lit - tle Lord
2. The cat - tle are low - ing, the Ba - by a - wakes, But lit - tle Lord
3. Be near me, Lord Je - sus, I ask Thee to stay Close by me for -

Je - sus laid down His sweet head. The stars in the sky___ looked
Je - sus, no cry - ing He makes. I love Thee, Lord Je - sus, look
ev - er, and love me, I pray. Bless all the dear chil - dren in

down where He lay, The lit - tle Lord Je - sus, a - sleep on the hay.
down from the sky, And stay by my cra - dle till morn - ing is nigh.
Thy ten - der care, And fit us for Heav - en to live with Thee there.

On Christmas Night

(Sussex Carol)

Traditional English, alt. [GKE]

Traditional English [WE]

Allegro moderato

1. On Christ-mas night, true Christ-ians sing, To hear the news__ the an-gels bring,
2. The King of Kings to us__ is giv'n, The Lord of earth__ and King of Heav'n;
3. So how on earth can men__ be sad, When Je-sus comes__ to make us glad?
4. From out the dark-ness have__ we light, Which makes the an-gels sing this night:

REFRAIN

News of great joy__ and of__ great mirth,
An-gels and men__ with joy__ may sing
From all our sins__ to set__ us free,
"Glo-ry to God,__ His peace__ to men,

Ti-dings of our dear Sav-ior's birth.__
Of blest Je-sus, their new-born King.__
Buy-ing for us our lib-er-ty.__
And good will, ev-er-more!__A-men."__

We Wish You a Merry Christmas

Traditional English

Traditional English [WE]

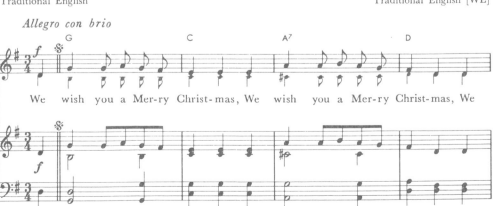

Allegro con brio

We wish you a Mer-ry Christ-mas, We wish you a Mer-ry Christ-mas, We

We Wish You a Merry Christmas
(continued)

From *The International Book of Christmas Carols* by Walter Ehret and George K. Evans © 1963 by PRENTICE-HALL, INC., Englewood Cliffs, New Jersey. Reprinted by permission.

wish you a Mer-ry Christ-mas, And a Hap-py New Year!

REFRAIN

Good ti-dings to you wher-ev-er you are; Good ti-dings for Christ-mas and a Hap-py New Year! We

Crafts to Deck the Hall

Butterfly

1.

2.

1. Fold a 4- × 4-inch square of thick red foil in half and cut out a butterfly, using pattern.

2. Cut out an identical shape in construction paper of a contrasting color. Cut butterfly shapes and patterns in this paper. Decorative gold glitter may be glued on if desired. Place decorated butterfly cutout on top of the foil cutout and staple together.

3. Bind the two pieces together by wrapping a pipe cleaner around them vertically to form butterfly's body. Allow the ends of the pipe cleaner to protrude from the head to form antennae.

4. Attach a green pipe cleaner to the underside of the butterfly for hanging.

3.

4.

5.

Robin redbreast

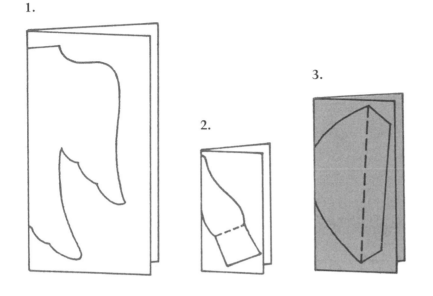

1. Fold a 5- × 5-inch square of black construction paper in half and cut out pattern A.

2. Fold a 2½- × 2½-inch square of black construction paper in half and cut out pattern B.

3. Fold a 3½- × 3½-inch square of red construction paper in half and cut out pattern C.

4. Fold and glue together A and B as indicated on pattern. In doing this, the straight portion of B will be inserted inside fold of A and only the curved portion of the head will protrude.

5. Fold tabs on C and glue to the underside of A as indicated on pattern. Glue should be applied only to the tabs of C. Then A and C can be flattened together.

6. To round out the bird's shape, gently press the center fold of C while pressing on the center fold of A.

7. Bend tail upward and decorate bird with glitter or paint. Thread may be attached to hang bird from tree.

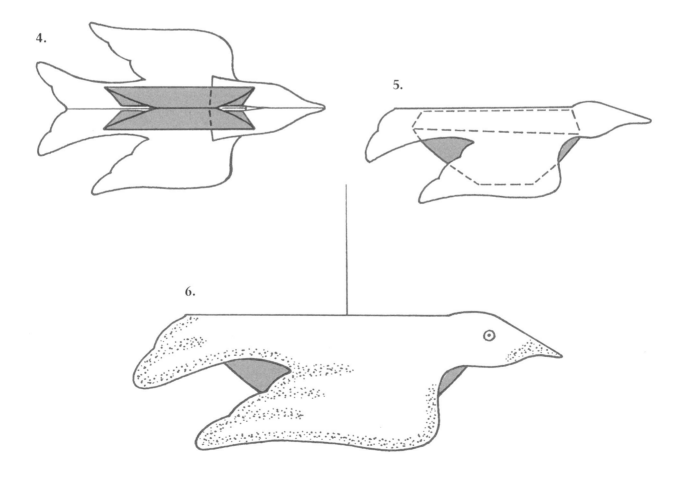

Welsh border fan

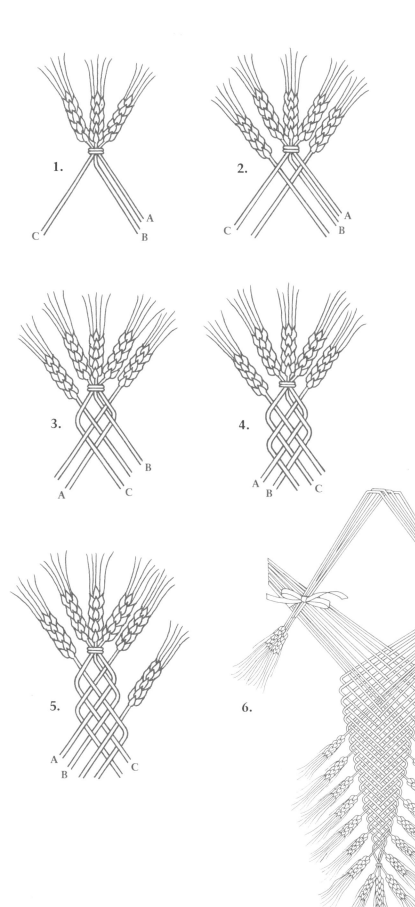

1.

2.

3.

4.

5.

6.

Select 21 straws of oats, wheat, rye, or barley. Soak them overnight to make them flexible for weaving.

1. Tie three straws together and spread them out. The straws will be A, B, C, from right to left.

2. Insert a straw under A and over B. Insert a straw under C and over the one already inserted.

3. Take A back and under B and let it lie to the left. Repeat the same with C, letting it lie to the right.

4. Repeat with outside right-hand straw and outside left-hand straw.

5. Insert a straw under the outside right-hand straw and over all other straws and let it lie to the left. Lock this into position by taking right-hand straw and repeating step 3, making sure that it passes under the outside straw and over the others.

6. Continue working from right to left, until you've used 17 straws. Note that as the work progresses the outside straw travels over an increasing number of other straws.

7. To finish off fan, tie the ends of the straws of each group together and trim off at an angle.

8. Tie the remaining four straws together and connect to other straws as shown. Ribbons may be used to join here if desired.

Concertina

1.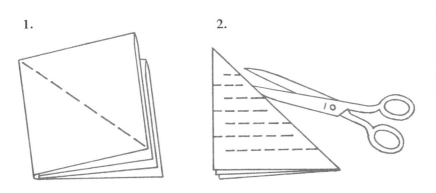

2.

3.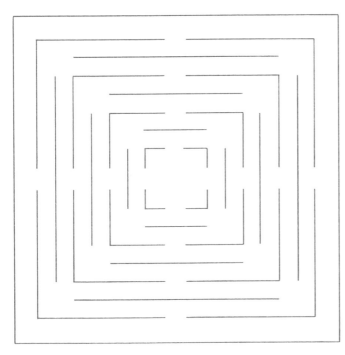

1. Cut a 7-inch square from red or green construction paper or other similar paper. Fold the square in half to form a rectangle. Fold this in half again, forming a small square. Then fold this diagonally to form a triangle.
2. With sharp scissors, make a series of cuts alternating from side to side. Each cut should end within $\frac{3}{8}$ inch of the opposite edge. The first cut should be made about $\frac{1}{2}$ inch in from the side and should begin on the folded edge of the triangle. The following cuts should be about $\frac{3}{8}$ inch apart.
3. After making all cuts, unfold the paper to its original size and straighten out creases by bending in opposite direction.
4. Repeat the above steps, alternating between red and green squares of paper, the number depending on how long you want the finished chain to be. Make sure all squares are the same size.
5. Staple or glue the finished squares together, joining corner to corner and center to center to form a chain.
6. Stretch the chain and hang across a wall or from a ceiling. Other lightweight decorations may be attached to this chain if desired.

4.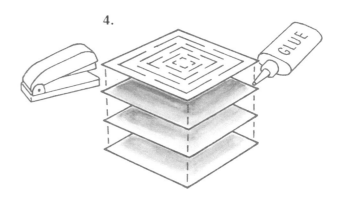

5.

Savouries of the Season

Roast potatoes

½ cup butter or margarine
8 large baking potatoes (about 4 pounds)
1 tablespoon seasoned salt
½ cup chicken broth

1. Melt butter in a 13- × 9-inch baking pan.
2. Pare potatoes; roll in melted butter to coat well. Sprinkle with seasoned salt.
3. Bake 1 hour at 350°F.
4. Turn potatoes and add chicken broth. Bake 30 to 45 minutes longer, turning occasionally.
8 servings

Brussels sprouts with almonds

2 pounds Brussels sprouts
1 beef bouillon cube
½ cup blanched almond halves
2 tablespoons butter or margarine
½ teaspoon salt
¼ teaspoon pepper
Few grains ground nutmeg

1. Cook Brussels sprouts until tender, adding bouillon cube to cooking water; drain off liquid.
2. Add almonds, butter, and seasonings to Brussels sprouts; heat thoroughly.
8 to 10 servings

Mincemeat

½ pound suet, finely chopped
1 cup sugar
2 cups dried currants
1 cup seeded raisins
1 cup golden raisins
½ cup diced mixed candied fruit
1 pound cooking apples, pared, cored, and finely chopped
½ cup chopped almonds
¼ teaspoon each cinnamon, mace, and nutmeg
Grated peel and juice of 1 lemon
¼ cup brandy or rum

Mix all ingredients in a large bowl. Cover and set aside in a cool place for at least 2 weeks.
About 1½ quarts

76

Mince pies

Mincemeat (about 1⅔ cups)

Rough puff pastry:
1½ cups all-purpose flour
½ teaspoon salt
¾ cup butter, cut in large chunks
1 teaspoon lemon juice
3 to 4 tablespoons cold water
Egg white, slightly beaten
Sugar for topping

1. Have mincemeat ready.
2. For pastry, mix flour and salt in a bowl; add butter and lemon juice. Add water gradually, mixing with a fork until a firm dough is formed; butter should remain in chunks. Cover and chill 15 minutes.
3. Roll pastry into a rectangle about ½ inch thick. Fold from ends toward center, making 3 layers. Turn one-fourth of the way around and roll into a rectangle about ½ inch thick. Fold again to make 3 layers. Refrigerate 15 minutes.
4. Repeat step 3 twice. Wrap dough and chill.
5. On a lightly floured surface, roll out a portion of pastry to about ⅛-inch thickness. Cut out eighteen 3-inch rounds. Roll remaining pastry to about ¼-inch thickness and cut out eighteen 3-inch rounds.
6. Put thin pastry rounds on cookie sheets and spoon about 2 tablespoons mincemeat on each; moisten edges of rounds, top with thicker rounds, and press edges together. Make a small hole in top of each. Brush tops with egg white and sprinkle with sugar.
7. Bake at 450°F. about 15 minutes, or until lightly browned. Cool.
18 pies

Apple yule logs

8 large cooking apples, pared and cored
1 cup soft breadcrumbs
½ cup finely chopped seeded raisins
¼ cup packed brown sugar
1 to 2 tablespoons Scotch whisky
¼ cup light corn syrup
¼ cup dark corn syrup
½ cup Scotch whisky

1. Arrange apples in two rows in a large baking dish.
2. Mix breadcrumbs, raisins, brown sugar, and a little whisky to moisten. Spoon into apple centers. Mix corn syrups. Pour over stuffed apples.
3. Bake 30 to 40 minutes at 325°F., or until apples are tender, basting frequently.
4. Pour syrup from dish into a small bowl.
5. Just before serving, warm the whisky, pour over the apples, and ignite. Serve apples with the sauce.
8 servings

Note: If desired, chill the apples before flaming.

Christmas pudding

1 cup all-purpose flour
½ teaspoon salt
½ teaspoon each cinnamon, nutmeg, and allspice
¼ teaspoon cloves
½ pound suet, finely chopped
2 cups fine dry breadcrumbs
1 cup sugar
4 eggs, slightly beaten
½ cup brandy or rum
¼ cup milk
Grated peel and juice of 1 lemon
1 cup chopped walnuts
1 cup currants
1 cup seeded raisins
¾ cup golden raisins
¾ cup diced mixed candied fruit

1. Sift flour, salt, and spices together.
2. Put suet, breadcrumbs, sugar, eggs, brandy, milk, and lemon peel and juice into a bowl; mix well. Stir in nuts and fruit. Add dry ingredients and mix well.
3. Turn batter into a thoroughly greased 2-quart mold. Cover tightly with a greased cover or tie on aluminum foil, waxed paper, or parchment paper.
4. Place mold on trivet or rack in a steamer or deep kettle. Pour boiling water into steamer to about one half the height of the mold. Cover. Steam pudding 4 hours. Add more boiling water if necessary during steaming.
5. Remove pudding from steamer and unmold on a serving plate. Serve with Hard Sauce.
About 16 servings

Hard Sauce: Cream ½ cup butter with 1 cup packed light brown sugar until fluffy. Add 2 to 3 tablespoons dark rum gradually, beating well. Chill.

Butter shortbread

2 cups sifted all-purpose flour
6 tablespoons sugar
2 tablespoons cornstarch
¾ cup butter

1. Sift flour, sugar, and cornstarch into a bowl. Cut in butter until mixture becomes a soft dough (requires working beyond the stage when particles are the size of rice kernels).
2. Shape dough into a ball; knead lightly with fingertips until mixture holds together.
3. Press into a buttered 8- or 9-inch round layer cake pan. Flute the edge. Prick dough thoroughly with a fork.
4. Bake 35 to 40 minutes at 350°F., or until lightly browned. Remove from oven when almost done. Mark into sections with a knife. Return to oven until baked.
5. Cool in pan.
8 to 10 pieces

Trifle

Sponge cake:
½ cup sifted cake flour
½ teaspoon baking powder
⅛ teaspoon salt
2 eggs
½ cup sugar
1 to 1½ teaspoons lemon juice
3 tablespoons hot milk
½ cup raspberry jam
½ cup slivered or sliced blanched
  almonds
1 cup sherry

Custard:
2 eggs
1 egg yolk
⅓ cup sugar
⅛ teaspoon salt
1½ cups milk
1½ teaspoons vanilla extract

Topping:
1 egg white
3 tablespoons sugar
1 cup whipping cream, whipped
2 tablespoons sherry
Candied fruit for decorating

1. For cake, sift flour, baking powder, and salt together. Set aside.
2. Beat eggs until thick. Add sugar gradually while beating until thick. Mix in lemon juice. Sprinkle dry ingredients over egg mixture about one fourth at a time; gently fold in until blended after each addition. Add hot milk all at one time and quickly mix just until smooth.
3. Turn batter into a greased (bottom only) 9-inch round layer cake pan.
4. Bake 15 to 25 minutes at 375°F., or until cake tests done.
5. Cool about 10 minutes in pan on a wire rack. Remove from pan and cool completely.
6. Split cake layer and spread raspberry jam between layers. Cut into pieces and put into a glass serving bowl. Sprinkle with almonds. Pour sherry over all. Set aside 30 minutes.
7. Meanwhile, for custard, mix eggs, egg yolk, sugar, and salt in top of a double boiler. Add milk and stir over boiling water about 10 minutes, or until mixture coats a spoon. Stir in vanilla extract. Cool slightly.
8. Pour warm custard over cake in serving bowl. Allow to cool.
9. For topping, beat egg white until frothy. Add sugar gradually, beating thoroughly after each addition. Continue to beat until stiff peaks are formed.
10. Spread egg white over whipped cream and gently fold together. Fold in sherry. Spoon over custard layer. Decorate with candied fruit. Chill.
8 to 10 servings

Fruitcake

4 cups all-purpose flour
2 teaspoons baking powder
3¼ cups dried currants (1 pound)
2¾ cups golden raisins (1 pound)
2 cups diced mixed candied fruit
  (12 ounces)
1⅓ cups candied pineapple chunks
  (8 ounces)
1 cup halved red and green candied
  cherries (8 ounces)
1 cup chopped blanched almonds
2 cups butter
2 cups sugar
8 eggs
½ cup brandy or rum

1. Sift flour and baking powder into a large bowl. Mix in fruit and nuts.
2. Cream butter and sugar. Add eggs, one at a time, beating well after each addition. Mix in fruit and nut mixture, then brandy.
3. Spoon batter into a thoroughly greased 10- × 3-inch springform pan.
4. Bake 2½ hours at 300°F., or until cake tests done.
5. Cool cake 30 minutes in pan on a rack. Remove from pan and cool completely.
One 7-pound fruitcake

Illustration Acknowledgments

Cover: Ian O'Leary, Tony Stone Images

2: Ian O'Leary, Tony Stone Images

5: World Book photo by Steve Hale

6: Susan McCartney

7: Mel Klapholz

8: (top) David H. Endersbee, Tony Stone Images (bottom) Bob Berger

9: Julian Nieman, Woodfin Camp, Inc.

10: Mel Klapholz

11: Julian Nieman, Woodfin Camp, Inc.

12: (top and bottom) Susan McCartney

13: Susan McCartney

14: British Tourist Authority

15: (top) Tony Stone Images (bottom) World Book photo by Steve Hale

16: Susan McCartney

18: Susan McCartney

20: Shostal

22: Mel Klapholz

23: Radio Times Hulton Picture Library

24: The Granger Collection, New York

25: Radio Times Hulton Picture Library

26: (top) World Book photo by Steve Hale (bottom) The Newberry Library, Chicago

27: The Granger Collection, New York

28: Mel Klapholz

29: Radio Times Hulton Picture Library

30: Radio Times Hulton Picture Library

31: Radio Times Hulton Picture Library

32: (top) The Granger Collection, New York (bottom) Radio Times Hulton Picture Library

33: Mel Klapholz

34: James Jackson, Tony Stone Images

36: George Rodger

37: (top) World Book photo by Steve Hale (bottom) Bob Thomas, Tony Stone Images

38: Bob Thomas, Tony Stone Images

39: (left) World Book photo by Steve Hale (right) Bob Thomas, Tony Stone Images

40: George Rodger

41: George Rodger

42: Susan McCartney

43: Susan McCartney

44: Susan McCartney

45: Mel Klapholz

46: Homer Sykes, Woodfin Camp, Inc.

48: George Rodger

49: (top) Homer Sykes © *Once a Year*, Woodfin Camp, Inc. (bottom) Radio Times Hulton Picture Library

50: Homer Sykes © *Once a Year*, Woodfin Camp, Inc.

51: Adam Woolfitt, Woodfin Camp, Inc.

52: Homer Sykes © *Once a Year*, Woodfin Camp, Inc.

53: Homer Sykes © *Once a Year*, Woodfin Camp, Inc.

54: Hallmark Historical Collection; Hallmark Cards

56: (top and middle) Hallmark Historical Collection; Hallmark Cards (bottom) Raphael Tuck and Sons Limited, Blackpool, England

57: (top) David Oakes Collection (bottom left and right) Hallmark Historical Collection; Hallmark Cards

58: Susan McCartney

60: British Tourist Authority

61: Antony Miles, Bruce Coleman, Inc.

62: British Tourist Authority

63: George Rodger

65: Radio Times Hulton Picture Library

72-75: Mel Klapholz